HERE'S PLENTY

poems

David Radavich

Červená Barva Press
Somerville, Massachusetts

Červená Barva Press

P.O. Box 440357

W. Somerville, MA 02144

www.cervenabarvapress.com

Bookstore: www.thelostbookshelf.com

Cover photo: A close up of apples on a tree by Markus Winkler

Production: Allison O'Keefe

ISBN: 978-1-950063-31-4

Library of Congress Control Number: 2023939796

For Anne,
my partner amid the leaves

CONTENTS

I.

II.

III.

IV.

V.

VII.

HERE'S PLENTY

I.

Sun Blanched

Eve's Garden, South Carolina

This is the fertile
garden I never knew.

Palm trees,
oracular birds
a noisy symphony,
breeze taking
notes of
an afternoon.

I can hardly believe
you're gone.

Children mount
their surfboards
eternally optimistic

before crashing
like the rest of us
against waves
of our own choosing.

Two men play
catch like dancers.

You didn't say good-bye.

Just silence
like the rippled
inlet, egrets
wading necessarily
through reeds.

Southern Living

The sun down here
is deep, and soul-wide.

Hiding is hard
but everyone tries—

big tales, small lies,
sunscreen, patio screen,
ballcap or parasol,

simply idling
with sweet tea once
the heat
gets so high

it kicks off socks
on its own.

You have to put down
deep, deep roots
in this soil

where old water
draws back

and memory
and pain are blended
cocoa and cream.

The oaktree knows
what has hung
in these branches,
how peckers sing
of nests and flying,

returning home
to roots,

what cools off
this burning heart.

Story-Telling

How come all my friends
speak in novels—

some of them published—

with great sprawling plots
and characters who claw
into your mind
returning from war,
betrayals and sex scenes
and tragic regrets
and more than enough
twists to overturn a house?

Beginning, middle,
flashback, re-start, end.

My sort merely
stroll along the sand
thinking on tides
and time,

relations that might have
been, and God,

and maybe turtles
who just now are turning
beach-ward to
lay their sudden eggs.

Civil War Canticle

The faces know each other.

Bodies worn and slumped,
families are divided as
after-dinner cakes
sliced and fought over.

Disease is everywhere:
in the feet especially,
in the crotch and lungs,
coughing and bleeding
till the last wheeze.

So many will never see home.

Now there are monuments
to fight over: who is
a hero, who betrayed,
what does history mean
when siblings eat
their ghostly, separate meals?

The fallen are still fallen.

Yet the past is not dead.
It rings insistently,
incessantly along the aisles
of churches built from
imaginary broken glass.

The former battlefields
grow green again with
tourists marching leisurely,
wearing goofy hats.

Some will rest in peace.
Others will turn over
and never speak the name
that hatred serves.

Slave Quarters

In Mississippi

This is where
they kept their chattel.

Where hail
on the tin roofs
felt like
a pale echo
of the real torture.

No chains in sight
but no beds, rotting wood,
windows boarded up,
smell of
damned living
sun-baked
in the humid walls.

Tourists can now
visit like ghosts,
stroll through
the gates,
even stay the night

and leave
with the wind
clutching their phones.

Somewhere near
a loved one was sold
like an arm,

a leg ripped off
for the fields
of the always reborn.

Grief doesn't
recognize colors
or flags
or slogans

or an afternoon
of eyes
walking in shame.

Untamed Wolfe

This is a man
who flummoxed people
with his gangly
flamboyant poems,

his big verbal strides
and refusal to go home,

let alone his slovenly
suit and eyes that pierced
every inquisitor
against a high frame.

Size was
how he walked
and where he lived.

No wonder this mountain
wind sweeps away
so much underbrush,

soars above valleys, roars
down ravines
then stops suddenly

where you or I might be

and hands over
a cocktail of words

that take away
all evening.

Vet

Don't imagine
the war is over

just because
you've come home.

Just because
your wounds
have been wrapped,

just because
there were crowds
in the streets

and a few
remembered.

The battle goes on

moon and memory
light and cloud

this morsel
this defecation

and having to
decide like a hawk.

No one can save you
from living.

Love is a shoal
in the river.

The front line
is today:

peace ringing

somewhere
in the blood.

II.

October Planting

Plastic boxes are lined up
like a platoon in the driveway.
We can only imagine
the forces they'll do battle
with. Mother says it's already
too cold for this. She's probably right.
A war they don't deserve
and may not come home from.
Such is life. And death.
Fully in the hands of others
who are indifferent or incompetent.
We put our backs to the task
nonetheless with sweat
and strategize like generals.
The ground heaves under
us in earthquakes of intention,
colors clash against blade,
a whole afternoon becomes
incursion into the deeper sanity
of nature without any self
or victories of time.

Garden Again

Apples, apples everywhere.
Orchard beside the road.

What are we meant
to know?

Is it still forbidden?

Will we need
to walk everywhere
hereafter
covered
and alone?

How round and red
they look.

Little sculptures
hanging
on a lamp.

Let me taste just
this one

and see
its inner light.

Crux

For Shelby

This is where
boy meets man:

a space
always alone

between
water and land,

fishing
or hiking,

gathering crayfish,
skipping stones,

another boss
is another tyrant,

pay not enough
to make ends meet,

mouths to feed
at the table,

gills in the water
needing your lure

and just the right
throw to home

sliding in
or head-long,

swinging high over
that creek

never knowing
if the vine will hold,

that's what being
adult means:

learning
not to trust,

pulling everything
you've got,

keeping a sharp eye on
what's moving

and then
grab it for grace,

feed that family
and don't apologize.

Lineage

Twin uncles:
one a lanky loner
who smoked himself
to death,

the other a diabetic
who refused treatment,
losing his legs,
his eyes,
and finally his heart.

How they both
somehow hated life,
or themselves
in it,

living a whole
continent apart
like bookends.

I never knew
either of them well
enough to call.

Once I borrowed
a car to make it home
from hell,

then silent
as men grieving.

We only saw
each other through
photographs

faded
and fingered

and a common
gene pool

stubborn as stone.

Thanksgiving

Umbrellas have all
gathered inside the door
like globed blossoms

in front
of a funeral.

Some of us
have arrived—

the rest
are here but
not here—

for joy as
we can claim it.

The holiday party
brings too much food

and forced
gratitude

some of us truly feel.

Grace in public
sings like
a chorister

in starched collar.

Under spines
by the door
tears drop away

from judgment,
mercy, forgiveness,

all the angers
of the house.

Ritual is not enough
in the end.

How practical
to bring our props
with us—

all the same props—

and let them
mingle

in the
entryway

as if they
could be friends.

Snow Bound

How thin and deep
the air is

like a
silver flute.

Noise is muted,
serene, without news,

without love
that doesn't feel
necessary.

Nothing appears
as it used to:

white, woolen.

This is what
birth remembers.

Rest, rest,
the red-tailed hawk
calls insistently.

As if humans
will listen

to a world
they half destroyed.

Legal Cession

Notwithstanding
the eight-inch snowfall,
my back is sore and humorless.

Heretofore
I found it manly
to tough out the shovel,

lift nature to
one side and arrange
white artfully along trim rows.

Thereunto
did I suffer from
vigorous man's delusion,

which appertaining
I now cede
mens in corpore

to the alienee
of youthful exuberance.

Hereinafter
shall the neighbor boy
who came knocking earlier

assume all future
rights and responsibilities

to the aforesaid
snow, ice,
and vertebrae.

Lost Vocabulary

It is a long list,
the words I have never
broken. The verbjerking, half-monkey,
lathe-pulling, sawtoothbiting adjectives
turned nouns
that bite
into the apple
then spread canopies
over the ears like sycamores
arced over the swimminghole where naked boys
remember jumping
past June bugs, river sedge,
sun devils, lost
in cold, cold water
folding over the body
of language I've forgotten
now, otters down mud-slides,
family behind tombstones,
ghosts real as pumpkins,
weeds grown up
majestic as sentences,
these great green crowns.

Canker Worms

These are the little suckers
who eat up all our trees
within a bald inch
of their lives every spring

as if they owned the natural
world—which they
do for a time—monarchs

of their own green
kingdom high above the floor
of pine-strawed shrubs
only partially attended
by the hand of man.

Females are the worst.
They can lay their five hundred
eggs in a toast to fertility
hardly any males can match.

I must say, I admire
their hunger, their thumbing
at the world of chance
undaunted by any odds,
relentless as the best of generals.

Whole neighborhoods can be
devoured—discreet, leafy streets
delight the most, it seems,
and owners there strain out
their bands and sprays
with furrowed brows like mice.

What drama plays out
each year and has us all
unnerved and poorer,

what power the minuscule
maintain over the big, those
with cell phones, designer jeans,
after-school appointments
and date-books full of
important networking events.

It's a torment to hate
these illegal immigrants,
who only want to make a living
at our expense and never got
any papers or permission
or even the silver greetings
of trees about to lose their grace.

III.

Charlotte Convention

I don't know where
you will find much history.

In museums,
in roped-off displays
and a few park-like estates
with docents and maps.

The real time
is only now

and we are living it
without shadow
like a 2-D
group of faces

trying to be upbeat,
trying to bc hip
and young and beautiful.

And we are

full of zeal now
with few memories,

but you'll notice many
pleasant streets

that curl
and rename themselves
with willow oaks
as sentinels

and only the civil war
that race remains

and class extremes
dividing neighborhoods
with an elected fence.

Somehow we were hornets*
at the beginning

and we're still
swarming

now and in the day
of our becoming.

* British General Cornwallis described Charlotte as a "hornet's nest of rebellion"
during the Revolutionary War.

Moon-Shot

Atlanta, 2014

It's still here

after a long
night of white
fullness
against the
black darkroom

now over
skyscrapers
busy with
capitalism,

a bit faint
behind clouds
yet still
noticeable

as a facemark

that moves
slowly
toward
meaning

and disappears.

Moscow Memory

For Akhmatova

I've never been there.

But that doesn't
stop me
from writing.

The unmarked streets,
weathered faces,
new gilt scabbarding
on rebuilt churches,

history without eyes
one can greet

or dance
alone in the dark.

Nowhere seems to be
everywhere

as I walk
to the center

where the towers
gather like
cruel saints in prayer.

The souls
who suffered here
sing like swallows still.

I can hardly
stand

to inherit
this dream.

Chicago Scene

Every time I see your face
I think of a beautiful woman,
confident, high-heeled,
briefcase in hand
on her way somewhere,
neat and firm as a clock,
almost German but with flair.

I don't take her out often,
I don't have that kind of money.

I sneak in, spend the night,
ruminate over morning coffee
then sail out under my own steam
to somewhere less challenging,

a woman with hills and curves,
fertile soil, the kind you curl up with
and know how to handle.

This city is not where nature
carries out her subtle art. The lake
restrains the travesties of man
as best it can.

Yet what artifice holds up
against the sky—

clouds hover and move
slowly: staying their rounds,
eyeing the winter glare.

Agape; Or, Sipping Coffee at Starbucks on a Saturday Afternoon

It is not easy
watching and feeling
the body waste
away

almost
without notice

the young
come strolling by
in their gaiety

touching
something deep
and eternal

something lost

cells aching
in the furnace

whose fire
rages

now at a distance

dancers
leaping lightly

in the mind

Commuting

There are no real
sunsets here: only trees

that lobster
and hang over

like fussing
but beloved aunts

on curving streets
up and down,

dizzily beautifying
everything

with slivers
of red sun: hard

symptom
of a day worked
to the bone,

mind fried in deep
commercial oil

and now

darkness
agglomerating

in leaves
that wrap us home

to be happy
in our chairs,

feet up like
salesmen calling

in their price.

Eden II

The trees in back belong
somehow to the city.

We look out at them
as steady saints—

beholden,
at a green remove—

and give thanks
we're also close to shopping,
the boxy needs of life

we keep
on a quiet leash,

sipping wine
on the deck, minding

grandchildren
and their errant balls

and just being
in sun

with airtrails
overhead

that take us
anywhere
we want to go—

IV.

Ode

I'm not sure
I can praise anything.

That seems
such a stretch—

approach the mountain,
approach the sea?

And then to speak
like an orator

wanting applause,
wanting to convince the air.

Don't the great things
sing themselves?

Words already know
what they mean,

whether high or low
their rank
among stars.

Save your poem
for the ghost
that's sure:

the forgotten
the oppressed
the never to be seen
again.

Offering

From one day
to the next
seems a difference

between drought
and flood,

corporations
and the poor.

Should we pack
our suitcase
for the future?

We bend over
gardenias
in the back yard,

salvia, rosemary,
daylilies just now
blazing

wondering if nature
can withstand
our age,

sun fighting
with wind and rain,

wars consuming
everything

we believe.

Time to visit
the cemetery, bring

the pure lilies
we picked
this morning

as our offering
to the dead.

We owe them
our knees
and this stab at

continuing

paying homage
to names

and all
that's green.

Climate Change

This year all the trees
and flowers bloomed early:

They make
a mockery of time,
and the sky is not ready.

Pollen floats in the air
before noses can be cleared
and Kleenexes bought.

Even love has to
catch up: bees scramble

ahead of rain,
birds call somehow
bewildered in the woods.

If this is always,
we're in trouble:

Spring will burn
our nostrils
and the moon will turn

orange

before any fall
before any harvest.

The Real You

Be careful what you buy.

It is the beginning
of relationship.

Difficult to divorce.

You must live
with your things

or someone else
must take their care.

They crowd up
the house

and colonize
your mind.

Every cat, every coat,
every Jaguar XKE,

your body
and your love

full-time
or on consignment.

The landfill
knows your life.

Crash

I imagine it will
end quietly

without a choir.

We've been expecting
so long it's not
a surprise.

Your face
is just as beautiful,

gardenia
still in bloom,

trees rustling such
a little.

Mail will not
be delivered today,

crime
will diffuse.

Air will choke
and my hand will

reach out
and clutch yours

going down

Unemployed

The only thing
I can withhold
is my body.

If there's nothing
to take home,
no living wage,

no mortgage
no health care
no schooling,

the fat cats
will need to eat
their own gold.

Work for sawdust
is a transaction
I refuse.

As the sun
goes down
alone

I can live
and breathe
my blood

so long
as it lasts.

Pietò

At a refugee center

His face is poised
as an olive

holding his
toffee-haired girl

for life,
for dear life.

In a handpicked
suit and tie

he looks sad
beyond relief

yet calm as silk,
soft beyond

the waters.

What tortures
have they endured,

what barbed wire
what gunfire

what walking
into hate and fear.

Unmistakable

across
a crowded room.

Here they cradle
in tight memory,

a sculpture

carved
in living flesh.

Caveat

Humans almost invisibly
grow to resemble
their enemies.

That means
we need to be careful

which nemeses
we choose.

Less bees
than tortoise,

not tyrants
but maybe moose.

Opposites
do attract
and intermingle
like forgotten selves
that get to know
one flesh.

A diamond
whose glare was coal.

Be generous
in your hatred:

You never know
what you'll become.

V.

Latin Lover

I want it to be violent
like the throat of a revolver
kissing and smoking.
Never mind your folds enveloping
like red carnations. Let me pretend
it's dangerous: You, a stranger,
clutch with terrorist claws.
You cry, a murderess
or a refugee. The forests
ring desperate and deep. Hostage
is too kind a word.

I tell you,
Put in the bullet:
I want to try your country.

The Color of Lies

Why can't we wait
to be torn open?

It comes fast enough:
the fierce fire
the relentless wind

those fingers of flesh
crawling over us

as if
ownership
could be debated.

The night has turned
dark again: which is to say
empty and visited.

A cat has rolled over
in the smoke

hoping
for a violation.

You can't arrive
soon enough.

And I can't
wait until now.

Planning Ahead

There's still a kiss
waiting for you.

Not that you
have forgotten—maybe
you have—but

it's here
in the air

and you can grab it
at the doorstep

without even
setting foot inside.

Sometimes
parting is too hasty,

you leave
a handkerchief
or suitcase
behind,

a toothbrush
with your taste still
on the bristles.

Maybe just a smell
in the empty wine bottle.

The final parting
can come later—

the calendar rings
in a few months—

for now

there are still items
not accounted

for, a few last
details that say

what we meant
for the future.

Over

It all burns away
like a torch.

Too much caring
turns the heart to stone.

I will not
sit at your bedside.

Your face
melts into snow.

Visitation

I never put
much faith in angels.

I guess it's the wings,
the false flying,

the too-good-to-be-true
wishes fulfilled

by supernatural
agency.

Blood always
seemed better, and body

parts that
ran and scraped
their knees
on merry-go-rounds.

Darkness
that grappled fears
to headstone,

eyes that dreamt.

But lately
here you've been:

ever-present
hardly flying

still as embers
steady as rain.

I can only ask
you to inhabit me.

Southwest

Your body
is as a cactus
not stirring
in wind.

Succulent
under spines,
sometimes
a bloom

scoring drought.

How do we go
from here

beyond the desert
blue in sun

arms aching
skyward
almost human?

Finger Painting

Now that I am
halfway home, or gone,

I think more
on the final things.

Not resurrection: Death.
The process of disintegration,
crown of thorns, spikes
into hands and feet.

Living in a fertile flat
land, finding green
gone to wind-torn stubble
and the prayers
of birds.

A woman is a cello
I hold for making music
before silence

Descends with its
mocking bow.

You have poured wine
which dies down the throat
of this glass
now fluted, half full.

Emptiness offers fulfillment,
promise. I toast the
sun setting,

Kiss this soil
about to rhythm itself
in the brown womb

Where fingers
grasp and scrape
what they can't contain.

Don't answer me
yes or no. Read the book,
chapter by chapter,
vellum if we're specially lucky.

Breathe by the grey wild
sea and sink walking in sand.

Peonies beget poems,
life after life,
end brings out beginnings.

Already
your hand shivers
patterns you taught me
to hold on to.

Wind, rain, soil:
Greet us
fleeting and asleep.

Hello. Good-bye.
Let us paint one another
as we go.

Southern Amour

There's no art
that can do justice—

line or shape, hue or hunched-
over form, blotch or eye-
catching arc

about to descend
across an open sheet—

or for that matter
no word

or phrase, whatever part
of speech to etch

what body
can sing of itself

in a quiet or busy or loud
mode of being once

the other
has crossed that

threshold: no green
or hairy or delicate description

beyond what
I cannot say even

in music
that formlessness

gives shape to
time thumping in the blood

and no lyrics but
adrenalin

and a cawing of crows

Once Again

Every time we re-enact
is not the same.

A different spring,
a different fall.

This once a red leaf
flutters down,
blood of yellow.

Sun turns at just
a slant, rain
comes
or doesn't.

You either answer
back and smile
or turn away.

Either way it's love—
bite of the apple,

a new road
walking home

with hands
that speak like birds.

Transfiguration

What we think we were—
an apple, lovers, democracy—
becomes something else,

digesting peel
and core, tyranny
or anarchy,

a tree being
chopped down
for a mall.

My face turns old,
yours remains
somehow

as I pictured it
sitting by the fire
at last light

reading what
becomes mind and soul
wrapped in a cloak—

a new day,
another meal,
someone else's life.

VI.

Token

Your shadow crept over
me as a face

going on a journey
I cannot join.

No surgery will fix this.
No soft words.

Telephone hangs
on its cord.

This is the way
into the bright darkness

where no
visitor returns.

Let me give you this peony
full of life's layers,

overflowing

hardly to keep this
whiteness of
a warm summer's night.

Self-Sufficient

For Audre

Imagine wandering
everywhere

with your bag
of magic.

Through the streets,
into forest—

who knows
what you will
pull out

to bless
or curse
the world?

Everything
you wear is
skin

in a woolen
onion.

Your hair
has seen no
restraint in years.

What if your hands
are crusted
as pies?

They still
express, command,
and soothe

like the mother
who was
a girl.

Somehow your eyes
match clouds.

Foretell the weather.
Foretell a way

of moving
still alone.

Prometheus on the Crag

It's someplace
I've come to feel
at home—

high above
air,

rocky as
all centuries,

seeing
everything

below me
in history,

torn each day
by talons

in the body's
red core,

fire burning
I know

like gods,
I share

with
everyone.

Listening to Shostakovich

It's the end of the world—
or maybe not.

You decide.

Secret police
record your every
thought—

but what thought!
Platonic and unrelenting.

Violins under the
celli, terrorist clarinets,

trumpets
announcing

more war dead.

Bombs strike
more than chords.

Eyes bloom everywhere.

At the same time
lushness

at its ease

sipping some dose
of aphrodisiac

to forget
to love

in a time of fear.

The fog hasn't cleared.

Abasement
by the state leads

the self
into perfect

clouds

suffering in air
a whole

century.

Going Home

Forget about it.

The old one wasn't
worth much
anyway.

You can do better
tossing a coin
or consulting
some astrologer.

Choose
where or what
you want to be

and go there
to take your place
among the yet
to arrive.

Wave your white
flag to the past

and make your new
garden bloom

as if
you had been

there all along
incognito

among many
creatures
you don't know
names for,

your enemies
forgotten

and a sky
just as much
your own

as a new skin.

Seaming

A duct under the house
pours out precious
conditioned air
into empty space.

One hole doesn't meet
another, emptiness
misaligned with emptiness,

so I lift the tube
and pound the nails
against black woven
hoists that seal the space.

I can't help thinking
of you in your IC room,
kept together with tubes
and monitors somehow
still cheerful about death
and life, which become
one in the very end,
emptiness joining with
emptiness till the tubes
carry forth what life
manages to seam together.

Yours is the brokenness
and I am no doctor,
but the house counts on
you as the foundation
that does not give way,
white as a bedsheet
tucked in night's basement.

My Twins

To call you
poetry and prose
is too simple.

You both sing,
both run off the page,
over the line,

images pour out
night and day,
mind and body,
sword and mother's milk.

Your map
has empty borders.

To nurture
is to be
a twin
somewhere

in this earth
of difference.

I call you into
writing like a bird.

Come, land on
my finger.

You alone
create the air.

Granddaughter's Right

She grabs my body
as if it were her own—

which of course
it is—

to grab, hug, poke
or ride on

round the shoulders
of the house

up stairs
behind sofas

weaving
like a fervent fish

or galloping
giraffe

high and holy

then ultimate
collapse

in giggles
and not a few

aches

that can only mean
life is plenty.

Still

This is the garden
we are born to.

With real toads
in it. Violence blooming
like trees, bursting

over houses,
in human hearts,

guns toted
with appendages
naked as sin.

Everywhere
a chorus of betrayal.

Yet still
the songbirds

sing, clouds pass
over, apples

ripen
in their red:

grief finds
a child

and brings a bright
doll in the night.

ACKNOWLEDGMENTS

The author would like to thank the editors and readers of the following publications in which individual poems from this collection have appeared:

"Crash" (rpt.) in *Best of the Friday Reading Series*
"Finger-Painting" in *Deus Loci*
"Caveat" and "Lost Vocabulary" in *Earth's Daughters*
"Listening to Shostakovich" in *Helen*
"Transfiguration" in *Intimacy* (anthology)
"Story-Telling" in *Iodine Poetry Journal*
"Legal Cession" in *J Journal*
"Pietò," "Self-Sufficient," and "Visitation" in *Kakalak*
"Commuting" in *Long River Run*
"Untamed Wolfe" (rpt.) in *Magic Again: Selected Poems on Thomas Wolfe*
"Climate Change" and "The Color of Lies" in *Main Street Rag*
"Charlotte Convention" and "Unemployed" in *The New Verse News*
"Chicago Scene" in *North Central Review*
"Slave Quarters" in *On the Veranda*
"Latin Lover" in *Poetz.com*
"Southern Living" in *Red Dirt Review*
"Moscow Memory" and "Vet" in *Section 8 Magazine*
"Offering" in *Third Wednesday*
"Untamed Wolfe" in *The Thomas Wolfe Review*
"Charlotte Convention" (rpt.) in *27 Views of Charlotte* (anthology)
"October Planting" in *What the Fiction?*
"Granddaughter's Right" in *What Matters* (anthology)
"Agape; Or, Sipping Coffee at Starbucks on a Saturday Afternoon"
        in *Wild Goose Review*

ABOUT THE AUTHOR

David Radavich is the author of two narrative collections, *America Bound: An Epic for Our Time* (2007) and *America Abroad: An Epic of Discovery* (2019). Among his lyric volumes are *Slain Species* (London, 1980), *By the Way: Poems over the Years* (1998), *Greatest Hits* (2000), and *Canonicals: Love's Hours* (2009). *Middle-East Mezze* (2011) focuses on a troubled yet enchanting part of our world, while *The Countries We Live In* (2014) explores inner and outer geographies. *Unter der Sonne / Under the Sun* (2022) features Radavich's German poems with English translations. *Here's Plenty* celebrates the sometimes searing yet ultimately redemptive richness of our planet and human experience.

Radavich's plays, both serious and comic, have been performed across the U.S., including six Off-Off-Broadway, and in Europe. He has published scholarly and informal essays and presented in such far-flung locations as Canada, Egypt, England, France, Germany, Greece, and Iceland. He has served as president of the Thomas Wolfe Society, Charlotte Writers' Club, and North Carolina Poetry Society and currently administers the Gilbert-Chappell Distinguished Poet Series.

HERE'S PLENTY COMMENTARY

At its heart, David Radavich's *Here's Plenty* evokes the American South—in all its messy, charming, baffling glory. As a microcosm of the fragile planet we inhabit, this region struggles with violence, poverty, racism, and outdated social convention. And yet the everrenewing beauty of the fertile landscape, a deep-seated love of story-telling, and the warmth of everyday people bring us the possibility of re-assessment and redemption. Radavich's poems embody the mesmerizing complexities of human life.

www.ingramcontent.com/pod-product-compliance
Lightning Source LLC
Chambersburg PA
CBHW021345090426
42742CB00008B/758